ROBOTS ON THE MOVE

WORLD BOOK

www.worldbook.com

Co-published by agreement between Shi Tu Hui and World Book, Inc.

Shi Tu Hui
Room 1807, Block 1,
#3 West Dawang Road
Chaoyang District, Beijing 100025
P.R. China

World Book, Inc.
180 North LaSalle Street
Suite 900
Chicago, Illinois 60601
USA

© 2026. All rights reserved. This volume may not be reproduced in whole or in part in any form without prior written permission from the publisher.

WORLD BOOK and the GLOBE DEVICE are registered trademarks or trademarks of World Book, Inc.

Library of Congress Control Number: 2025938166

Robots
ISBN: 978-0-7166-5814-6 (set, hard cover)

Robots on the Move
ISBN: 978-0-7166-5818-4 (hard cover)

Also available as:
ISBN: 978-0-7166-5828-3 (soft cover)
ISBN: 978-0-7166-5838-2 (e-book)

WORLD BOOK STAFF

Writer: William D. Adams

Editorial

Vice President
Tom Evans

Senior Manager, New Content
Jeff De La Rosa

Associate Manager, New Content
William D. Adams

Content Creator
Elizabeth Huyck

Proofreader
Nathalie Strassheim

Graphics and Design

Senior Visual Communications Designer
Melanie Bender

Photo Editor
Rosalia Bledsoe

ACKNOWLEDGMENTS

Cover: © 35lab/Shutterstock; © Zipline; © Boston Dynamics; © Nauticus Robotics
4-5   © Zipline
6-7   © Andrei Kholmov, Shutterstock; © Agility Robotics
8-9   © SuperDroid Robots; © Science Photo/Shutterstock
10-11 © E&K Automation; AGV Expert JS (licensed under CC BY-SA 3.0)
12-13 © INDEVA; © Amazon.com, Inc.
14-15 © LEGOLAND
16-17 © Boston Dynamics; NASA
18-19 © Boston Dynamics
20-21 © STR/AFP/Getty Images
22-23 © Half Point/Shutterstock
24-25 © F11 Photo/Shutterstock
26-27 © Liquid Robotics; © Yara
28-29 Elizabeth Crapo, NOAA Corps
30-31 © Nauticus Robotics
32-33 © University of Tübingen
34-35 © ID1974/Shutterstock
36-37 © Waymo; © Velodyne LIDAR
38-39 © Metamorworks/Shutterstock
40-41 © Jasper Juinen, Bloomberg/Getty Images
42-43 © 1000 Words/Shutterstock
44-45 John F. Williams, U.S. Navy; © Vaughn Youtz, ZUMA Press/Alamy Images
46-47 © Danvis Collection/Alamy Images; © Bob Collet, Alamy Images

Contents

- **4** Introduction
- **6** Moving Around
- **8** Rolling Robots
- **10** Driverless Delivery
- **12** Automated Navigation
- **14** AGV's Outside the Warehouse
- **16** Walking Robots
- **18** HELLO, MY NAME IS: Atlas
- **20** Flying Robots
- **22** Eyes in the Sky
- **24** Jobs for Drones
- **26** Robots at Sea
- **28** Diving Robots
- **30** HELLO, MY NAME IS: Aquanaut
- **32** I Get Around: Robotic Navigation
- **34** Aircraft Autopilot
- **36** Self-Driving Cars
- **38** Degrees of Self-Driving
- **40** Baby Steps or Giant Leaps
- **42** Where Does the Buck Stop in a Self-Driving Car?
- **44** DARPA Challenges
- **46** Hands-On Robotics
- **48** Glossary and Index

Terms defined in the glossary are in type **that looks like this** on their first appearance on any spread (two facing pages).

introduction

Robots are machines that sense their environment, decide how to act, and then—move. Some robots don't move much. They might swing an arm to fit parts together in a factory, or roll back and forth to inspect car parts. Many **industrial robots** are fixed in place, doing the same job day after day within a small circle. But other robots need to get around.

There are *mobile* (movable) robots that can roll, walk, fly, slither, and swim. They perform all kinds of tasks, from moving goods around factories to exploring other planets. Some deliver emergency supplies or inspect buildings. Soon they may deliver pizza or drive us to work and school.

In this book, you'll read about the different kinds of mobile robots. You'll learn about the challenges they have to overcome. You'll also meet some mobile robots and find out about how they do their jobs.

Mobile robots are good at reaching difficult places. The company Zipline uses **autonomous drones** to deliver blood transfusion supplies to areas with poor road networks, saving lives.

Moving Around

Not all robots need to move. Many do their jobs well while being bolted in place. For example, in a **structured environment** such as a factory, parts that an **industrial robot** work on usually come to it on a conveyor belt. Having the robots move around too would only make things more complicated.

Robots stuck in one place—such as these industrial robots—can be quite useful. But it is not always possible to bring the work to the robot.

Mobile robots face more challenges than their couch-potato cousins. But when it comes to getting the job done, mobile robots are really going places!

But many robots have to move around to accomplish their goal. Some move goods around warehouses or bring parts to other robots in factories. Others work in more **unstructured environments,** exploring land, sea, and even other planets!

Mobile robots must overcome many challenges not faced by immobile robots. An immobile robot must only keep track of whatever is in the area it can reach (called its **work envelope**). A mobile robot must figure out where it is, keep track of objects around it, and decide how best to move to get to where it's supposed to go. That's a lot!

[7]

Rolling Robots

All robots have **actuators** (usually motors) and **effectors.** In mobile robots, at least one of their actuators powers an effector that moves it through the environment. For most mobile robots, their effectors are wheels or **endless tracks.** Wheels make a robot fast and maneuverable over solid, flat surfaces. Endless tracks are usually better in rough, slippery terrain and in other places where the robot needs a lot of **traction.** Wheels are usually cheaper and easier to maintain than endless tracks.

Omni wheels
Using just three omni wheels, this robot can travel in any direction at any angle. The rollers along the edge of an omni wheel allow it to slide over the ground.

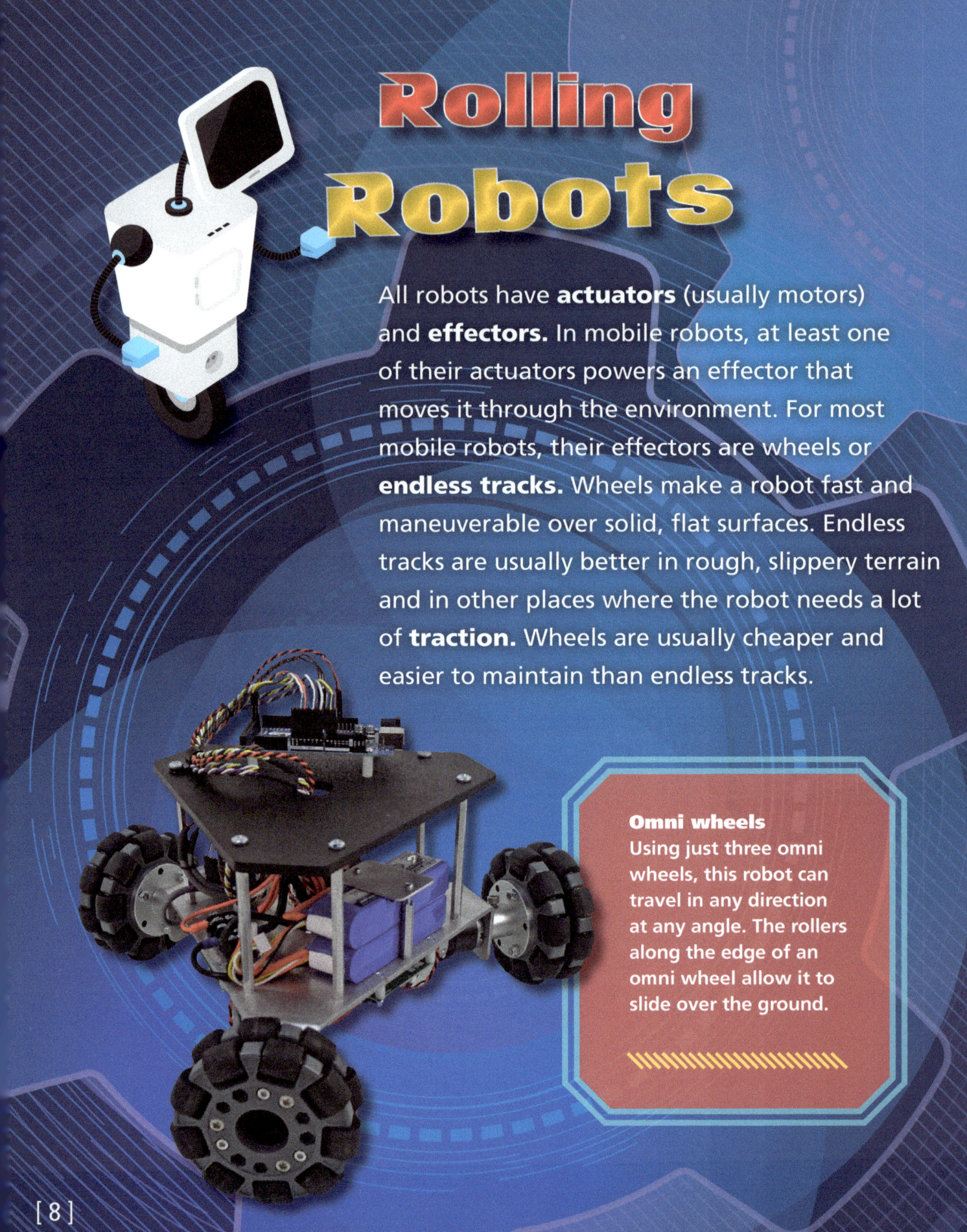

Endless tracks, endless fun
This robot uses endless tracks to get around, giving it plenty of traction over many kinds of surfaces.

Omni wheels are a special kind of wheel that allow for great flexibility. An omni wheel is a wheel with rolling spools mounted along its edge. Why is this useful? Traditional wheels create friction with the ground. When a vehicle with ordinary wheels wants to turn, it must first get the wheels pointing the direction it wants to go. With omni wheels, the 'bot can move sideways even if the main wheel is pointing forward. Robots with omni wheels can roll in any direction: forwards, backwards, sideways, or diagonally. But omni wheels can also slip more, so they can be a drawback when the robot needs a lot of traction.

Driverless Delivery

The most common wheeled robots in use today are **automated guided vehicles (AGV's)** and **autonomous mobile robots (AMR's).** They mostly work in such **structured environments** as warehouses and factories. AGV's follow guided paths along set routes. AMR's are more autonomous. Both come in many sizes and shapes, depending on the loads they have to move. Many are designed to work with standard shipping pallets.

"10-4, good buddy!"
A convoy of AGV's hauls pallets of canned beverages in a warehouse.

Clamp AGV's can move and stack large rolls of material. This one is moving huge rolls of paper.

Towing vehicles—also called tuggers—push or pull carts of materials. They can be many cars long and haul tens of thousands of pounds or kilograms. **Automated** forklifts work just like their crewed counterparts. They slide long metal forks under a pallet packed with merchandise to pick it up and move it to a different location. Drive units fit under shelves and containers to move them around a warehouse. Clamp AGV's use special grippers to grab loads that are not on pallets. Many are designed to pick up huge rolls of material, such as paper or metal.

Automated Navigation

Automated guided vehicles (AGV's) are a bit like a city bus—they travel a set route over and over. Early models followed electric signals from wires buried beneath the warehouse floor. Today, many AGV's follow taped paths on the floor. The tape is either magnetized or colored with a special pattern. **Sensors** on the bottom of the AGV detect the tape and drive along it to where it needs to go. Floor tape is much easier to install and change than buried wires. Some AGV's also navigate by bouncing **lasers** off special reflective tags placed around the space.

Let's go to the tape! These AGV's find their way around a warehouse by following magnetic tape laid out on the floor.

Small but mighty
The online retailer Amazon builds its own robots for its warehouses. Proteus is a fully **autonomous** mobile robot drive unit. Over half a million robots are in use in Amazon warehouses around the world, most of them drive units like Proteus.

Autonomous mobile robots (AMR's) move around more freely. They navigate with the help of optical sensors, **lidar,** and detailed maps of the work space, similar to a self-driving car. Most AGV's and AMR's are also equipped with proximity sensors to avoid collisions with other 'bots or human workers. AMR's allow more flexibility in factory and warehouse settings that frequently change.

[13]

AGV's Outside the Warehouse

Not all **AGV's** have boring jobs. Some drive in theme parks! In indoor rides called ghost trains or dark rides, riders board a car that takes them along a route filled with special effects, animatronics, and video displays. Often these cars travel on tracks. But around 2000, ride designers began using AGV's to make more flexible and fun dark rides. This allows cars to cross paths, take different routes, or move in different ways based on the actions of its passengers. The ride is also smoother. Today, dark rides with AGV's thrill people all over the world.

In the 1990's, some large office buildings used AGV's to deliver mail to workers. An AGV would stop at fixed spots on a route near workers' desks. After a certain amount of time, the mail-bot would move on to its next stop. The rise of email put mail-bots out work, so AGV and **AMR** units now deliver coffee and snacks.

Free to roam
In many modern amusement rides, such as the Lego Factory Adventure, visitors travel in AGV cars that don't need a track. The cars follow RFID (radio-signal) chips in the floor and walls to navigate the ride.

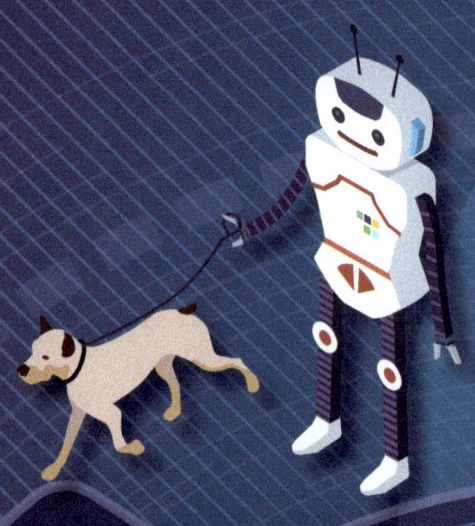

Walking Robots

Sometimes, wheels and **endless tracks** just don't cut it. If a robot needs to climb stairs or step over rocks, it might need to learn to walk.

Walking with two legs is actually very difficult—so give yourself a pat on the back! It's a little like controlled falling: If we were to stop moving our legs midstride, we'd fall over. Humans constantly make small adjustments—most without even thinking—to keep our balance while walking.

For a robot to walk on two legs requires dozens of powerful **actuators** and a super-fast

See Spot walk
Boston Dynamics's SpotMini is a four-legged robot that has no trouble with stairs. SpotMini can climb over all kinds of obstacles without missing a step.

computer to constantly make complex calculations. It took many years before roboticists were able to build and program a robot that walked even a bit well. But now more and better walking robots appear every year.

For many jobs, robots with four or six (or more) legs are better than two-legged models. Multilegged robots are more stable and use less computing power than bipedal walking robots. Four- and six-legged robots always have at least three legs on the ground at once, so they can stop midstride without falling over. They can also carry heavy loads, and many can climb stairs.

The right stuff
Robotic astronauts like NASA's Valkyrie might travel to space with or ahead of human astronauts to help with space missions.

HELLO, MY NAME IS:

Atlas

Atlas is one of the most advanced **humanoid** robots in use today. The first model was designed for the DARPA Robotics Challenge in 2013 and 2015 (see pages 44-45). Since then, it has been continuously improved. It can perform acrobatic stunts, carry heavy loads, run, and keep its balance when pushed. If it does fall over, it can get back up on its own. Atlas is designed to work in factories or to aid in rescue or emergency situations.

AUTONOMY

Medium to High

Atlas can be programmed to perform set tasks or act autonomously.

MAKER

Atlas is made by the American company Boston Dynamics.

SIZE

5 feet (1.5 meters) tall, 196 pounds (89 kilograms)

I DON'T MIND

Boston Dynamics sometimes posts videos of engineers messing with Atlas by tripping or pushing it. This doesn't irritate the robot—robots have no feelings! Boston Dynamics does this to show that their robots can respond to unexpected events.

Flying Robots

Robots don't just roll and walk around. Some fly! Flying robots don't need to worry about stairs or difficult terrain. But weight is a big consideration when designing a flying robot. The heavier it is, the more power it uses and the harder it is to fly around obstacles.

Flying robots also need lots of computing power. A robot rolling around on the ground doesn't need to worry about what is above or below it, but a flying robot does. Although there are fewer obstacles to navigate in the air, hitting them is much more dangerous. In the air, both the robot and other flying objects it might meet—such as birds or drones—are likely to be moving quickly, making fast reaction times even more critical.

"Where we're going we don't need roads." In 2024, the Ehang EH216-S became the first **autonomous** passenger **drone** to be approved to carry people, in Guangzhou, China. Several other companies are also working on robot air taxis to ferry people short distances.

Eyes in the Sky

Uncrewed aerial vehicles (UAV'S), often called **drones,** are small flying machines. Some are remote-controlled by a person, but others can be programmed to fly autonomously.

Drones perform all kinds of tasks. They study climate, examine crops, and take video of events. They can look for lost hikers and deliver emergency supplies. Militaries use large drones equipped with weapons to attack enemies.

The simplest drones are remote-controlled by a nearby human pilot. Remote-piloted drones are easier to build and program, because a human does the complicated navigating and steering.

In some places, laws require that a drone always be in sight of a human operator, even if it flies autonomously.

Birds-eye view
A warehouse worker uses a remote-control drone that can easily check pallets stored on high shelves.

Jobs for Drones

Fully **autonomous drones** and other robotic aircraft have many uses in construction, safety inspections, farming, and wildlife conservation. They can inspect bridges for flaws in places it is hard for people to reach. They can fly over remote areas to count wildlife. Some even work with other robotic equipment. A drone might fly over a farm field to check crop growth, mapping areas that need water or fertilizer. Based on these maps, the drones could send instructions to autonomous weeders or tillers to tend just the areas that need help.

Swarms of drones can also put on spectacular light shows, as a less-polluting alternative to fireworks. In choreographed drone shows, hundreds or thousands of small, lit-up, autonomous drones fly together to make pictures based on designs from human artists. They can also be used indoors as part of stage shows.

It's all fun and games, so far
Autonomous drones can be used to put on fantastic light shows, as in this heart-shaped display.

Robots at Sea

Robots can walk, roll, fly—but can they swim? Some do, both above and below the waves.

Fleets of small floating and swimming robots at the water's surface are being used to monitor ocean conditions, track plastic pollution, and warn of storms. These aquatic robots operate for long periods far out to sea, where it is impossible to plug in and recharge or change batteries. Most use solar panels or wind and wave power to move and power their onboard electronics.

Autonomous cargo ships may soon take over another boring job, hauling containers full of freight across the ocean. Autonomous ships are already being used as ferries and to carry cargo short distances. Longer voyages may soon follow. Shipping companies hope that autonomous ships will help speed up the transport of goods, prevent accidents at sea, and save energy.

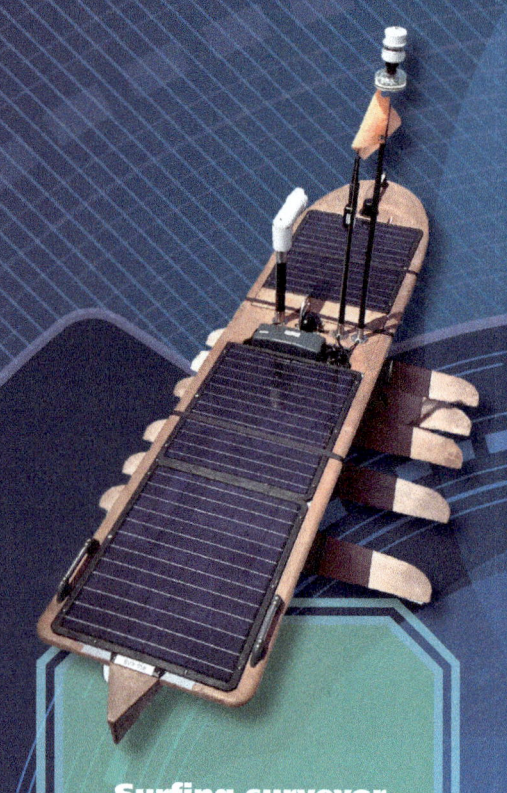

Surfing surveyor
This swimming robot, called WaveGlider, uses wave energy and solar power to move around the ocean. It can collect data on ocean conditions, spot ship traffic, and relay information from robotic submarines.

The Yara Birkeland is a fully autonomous electric-powered cargo ship in Norway. It ferries fertilizer from a factory to the nearby port.

Diving Robots

Under the ocean is a challenging place for humans. The water pressure is intense, and it is cold and dark. But aquatic robots called **autonomous** underwater vehicles (AUV's) can work under water without putting people in danger. AUV's usually have propeller **effectors,** but some have sails or even swim like fish!

AUV's are often used to survey the sea floor for places that might have useful resources, such as oil and natural gas. Other AUV's inspect underwater cables and pipes for signs of damage. Some help with underwater construction and repairs.

AUV's have played a big part in mapping the ocean floor and exploring underwater geological features, such as hydrothermal vents. They have also been used to find shipwrecks and monitor ocean wildlife.

One AUV, called RangerBot, patrols the Great Barrier Reef, off the coast of Australia. It monitors the health of the reef and has even been trained to spot and kill invasive crown-of-thorns starfish, which eat coral.

The Eagle Ray (front, just below the water's surface) is a United States AUV that can measure water conditions, map the sea floor, or spy on enemy submarines.

[29]

HELLO, MY NAME IS:

Aquanaut

Aquanaut is a real-life transformer! With its shell closed, it can speed through the water to a work site. Then the shell opens up to reveal robotic arms that extend to allow the robot to pick up objects, repair underwater machinery, and do other tasks.

AUTONOMY

HIGH

Because radio signals don't travel well under water, Aquanaut is designed to navigate to work sites and do tasks on its own.

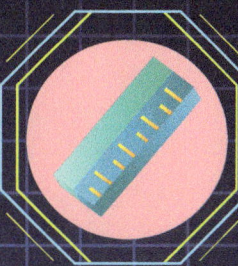

SIZE

Aquanaut is big enough to handle tough jobs, 11.5 feet (3.5 meters) long, weighing 2,315 pounds (1,050 kilograms).

ALL-IN-ONE

Aquanaut functions as both a speedy submarine (when closed) and a robotic arm (opened up). It is packed with sensors, cameras, sonar, GPS, and custom vision sensors for underwater navigation. It runs on rechargeable batteries, with a top speed of 8 miles (13 kilometers) per hour.

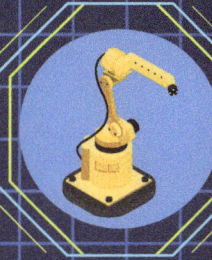

MAKER

Aquanaut is made by the American company Nauticus Robotics, founded by former NASA roboticists.

[31]

I Get Around: Robotic Navigation

To move around its environment, a mobile robot needs to keep track of both the environment and its location within it.

Mobile robots in **structured environments** usually rely on a map of their work area loaded into their memory. The work area may also have landmarks, such as reflectors or transmitters, scattered around so the robot can easily figure out where it is.

But if a robot doesn't have a map of where it is, how is it to figure out where it's supposed to go? Most use a method called "simultaneous localization and mapping," or SLAM. The robot uses **sensors** to map the environment around it. It then moves in the direction that most likely will allow it to achieve its goal. All the while, it continues to scan the environment, adding to its map and updating its place in it.

Researchers in Germany outfitted a simple **drone** with cameras and a powerful computer. It used SLAM techniques to map its laboratory as it flew around.

Aircraft Autopilot

All large passenger airplanes have a great deal of **automation** built into them. It keeps passengers and crew safe, saves fuel, and makes the pilot's job easier. Autopilots have been around for almost as long as airplanes. Early mechanical systems used a gyroscope to keep the plane on a level heading without the pilot having to constantly adjust the steering. Modern computer autopilots make constant tiny adjustments to the plane so it stays on course. This result in a smoother, more fuel-efficient ride. Many autopilots are also programmed to catch pilot errors. They can even land the plane if there are visibility problems, such as heavy fog.

Human pilots still manage most takeoffs and landings, and they take over if the plane encounters *turbulence* (when air disturbances cause the plane to bounce and shake). But fully robotic airplanes may soon ferry cargo—and after a while, people—through the skies.

Who's flying the plane?
If you have ever flown aboard a commercial passenger plane, odds are that autopilot took the controls for part of the journey.

Self-Driving Cars

One of the fastest-growing fields in robotics is **autonomous** vehicles. Autonomous vehicles have the potential to revolutionize how we get around.

Self-driving cars use an array of **sensors** to identify obstacles. One of these is **lidar,** which stands for *l*ight *d*etection *a*nd *r*anging. In a lidar unit, dozens of **lasers** send pulses of **infrared** light into the

Lidar units are often placed atop self-driving vehicles, such as in this test car from the company Waymo. From its perch, the unit can spin to see all around the car.

Lay of the land
This image shows what a lidar scan looks like. The lidar unit is in the middle of the black circle. Sounding the distances around it reveals the ground, cars, and trees.

environment. When the light bounces off objects and surfaces, sensors in the lidar unit detect the returning light. The longer the light takes to bounce back, the farther away the object is. The car's computer uses this information to get a picture of what's around it.

Lidar is useful, but it is quite expensive, and it can be confused by rain or snow. So most autonomous cars also use an array of cameras to see where they are.

[37]

Degrees of Self-Driving

Almost every car today has cruise control, where the driver can press a button to keep the car traveling at its current speed without having to keep a foot on the gas pedal. Some cars have systems that allow them to park automatically, or that apply the brake if the car gets too close to an obstacle. Are these cars **autonomous?** Because cars can have different levels of **autonomy,** experts have come up with a six-level scale:

- Level 0: No autonomy. A person controls all parts of driving.

- Level 1: Limited autonomy. A person controls most parts of driving, but the car may handle steering, acceleration, or braking in certain situations, such as when parking or in an emergency.

- Level 2: Partially autonomous under limited conditions. The car steers, accelerates, and brakes in some driving situations, but a person must watch the road and drive much of the time.

- Level 3: Fully autonomous under limited conditions, such as on a highway. A human driver must be ready to take over at any time.

- Level 4: Fully autonomous in a particular area. This type of car might take a passenger anywhere in a city, for instance, but nowhere outside of it.

- Level 5: Fully autonomous. A passenger could punch in any destination reachable by road.

Don't try this at home
Right now, reading in the driver's seat is a good way to get into an accident. But soon, cars may let us relax as they take us where we want to go.

Baby Steps or Giant Leaps

Different manufacturers are taking different approaches to developing fully autonomous vehicles. Some companies are gradually adding more safety and convenience features with each new model. With this "baby steps" approach, cars will become more autonomous over many years until they are fully self-driving. This allows people to get comfortable with self-driving cars over time. But, it may also lead them to overestimate what their vehicles can do.

Other companies are adopting a "giant leap" approach, aiming to create a fully autonomous car all at once. Such vehicles might have no steering wheel, pedals, or dashboard. But creating fully autonomous cars is challenging and very expensive. These cars may also still need help from remote human operators, who can view the car's video feed and guide the car by remote control when it encounters an unexpected situation. That might make the robotic cars more expensive than simply having a car with a human driver.

Fast or slow?
This car can take the wheel on highways—so long as the driver remains alert and ready to take control. But, if a driver expects the car to completely drive itself and stops paying attention, it may lead to accidents. Does that mean it would be better to go straight to a car with no steering wheel at all?

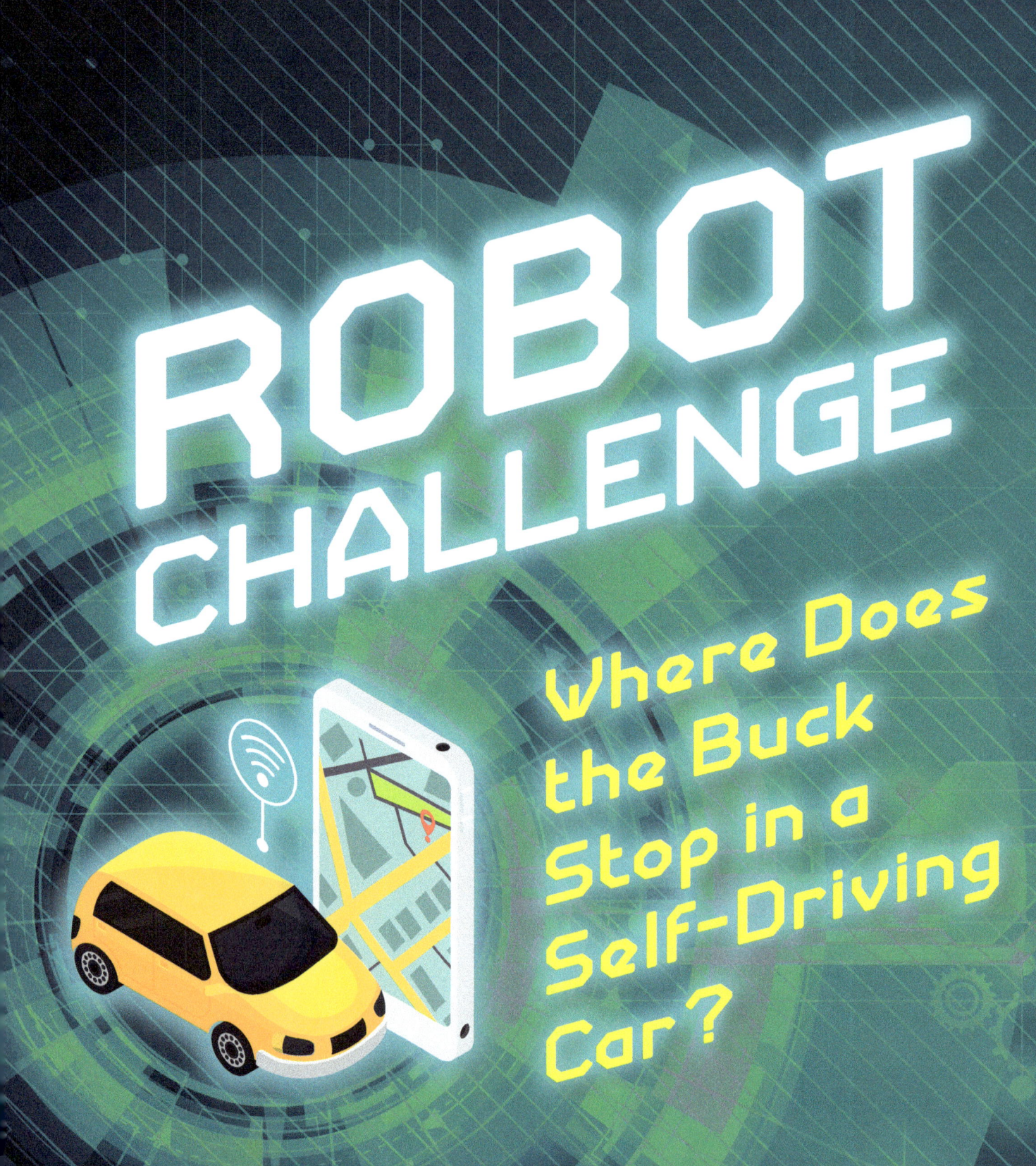

Self-driving cars have the potential to reshape our world. These changes will raise tough questions. The first concerns accidents. Who is responsible if a self-driving car hits a pedestrian? The owner of the car? The maker of the car? The programmers of the car's **software?** Or the car itself? Some makers of self-driving car systems have already stated that they will take responsibility in the event of a crash.

Another question is whether a self-driving car should prioritize the safety of its passengers. Does it protect them at all costs? Or does it risk hurting them to keep from hitting pedestrians or other vehicles?

Who will benefit from self-driving cars? People may use cars more if they don't have to drive, resulting in more traffic and pollution. Self-driving cars will benefit richer countries, where driving is already safer. Poorer countries, which usually have more dangerous roads and fewer safety laws, likely would not see self-driving car technology for many years.

Robot gridlock
Will self-driving cars help reduce traffic congestion, or will they make it worse?

DARPA Challenges

The Defense Advanced Research Projects Agency (DARPA) is a United States government organization that works to create and use new technology. In the late 2000's, it began hosting contests where scientists and engineers competed to solve difficult problems. Some of DARPA's most important contests have involved robotic mobility.

DARPA sponsored two Grand Challenges for autonomous vehicles in 2004 and 2005, and

Watch out for those turns! A walking robot navigates the course during the Robotics Challenge finals in 2015.

[44]

an urban driving Challenge in 2007. DARPA wanted to make U.S. military vehicles **autonomous** to keep more soldiers and military personnel safe. But at the time, no major companies were interested in autonomous vehicles. So DARPA sponsored a contest open to anyone.

Not a single team managed to complete the course in the first challenge, so DARPA hosted a second one in 2005. Many groups who participated in these challenges went on to found the self-driving car industry.

In 2013 and 2015, DARPA hosted a Robotics Challenge to build autonomous robots capable of working in dangerous environments. Challenges included traveling over uneven ground, climbing stairs, punching through a wall, and turning handles.

Road warriors
Five autonomous vehicles completed the 2005 Grand Challenge. Sandstorm (above) took second place, completing the 132-mile (212-kilometer) course in just over seven hours. But not every vehicle was able to finish the race. Spirit (below) got stuck in a patch of sand.

[45]

Hands-On Robotics

Want to get started making robots? Jump right in!

SeaPerch

If you dream of exploring the ocean with your very own robot submersible, SeaPerch can help you get started.

SeaPerch is an organization that teaches kids 10-18 to build their own custom underwater ROV (remote-operated vehicle) using a simple kit. The 'bots can be modified and programmed to do exploration, rescue, water sampling, or other tasks. The basic 'bot is built from PVC pipe, wiring, and zip ties. Then the creative engineering starts. What will yours look like?

For the SeaPerch competition, teams first compete locally in an underwater task challenge. The best from each region go on to an international competition.

The SeaPerch program is part of RoboNation, an international organization that hosts a variety of robot-building challenges and workshops for students. Other projects focus on autonomous aerial vehicles, boats, and submarines.

Pool party
Students test out builds in a pool (above) and ready their underwater robots for a competition (right) at SeaPerch.

Also check out:
- RoboNation challenges: SeaGlide, RoboBoat, RoboSub, RoboX
- MATE ROV competition
- National Underwater Robotics Challenge

Or ask at your local school, library, or maker space.

Glossary

actuator a device, such as a motor, that provides movement to a robot.

automated guided vehicle (AGV) a mobile robot that follows wires, tape, or markers to move items or people around.

automation the use of machines to perform tasks that require decision making.

automous mobile robot (AMR) a self-driving mobile robot that can navigate independently.

autonomy the degree to which a robot can make decisions without input from a human operator to achieve a goal.

drone an uncrewed aerial vehicle. Many drones are piloted remotely, but some are autonomous.

effector the part of the robot's body, such as a wheel or a gripper, that is moved by an actuator and interacts with the environment to perform an action.

endless tracks a long tread stretched between two or more wheels on which a vehicle moves, instead of tires.

humanoid shaped like or resembling a human.

industrial robot a robot that works in a factory to help create a product.

infrared light that has wavelengths longer than those of the red part of the visible spectrum and shorter than those of microwaves.

laser a device that produces a very narrow and intense beam of light of only one wavelength going in only one direction.

lidar a sensing method in which pulses of laser light are used to measure distances and create three-dimensional pictures of an environment.

omni wheel a wheel with rolling spools mounted along its edge to reduce its friction with the ground and allow it to slide in any direction.

sensor a device that takes in information from the outside world and translates it into code.

software a general term for computer programs. A computer program is mostly made up of a sequence of instructions. The instructions tell a computer what to do and how to do it.

structured environment in robotics, an area in which a robot operates that has been specially designed to reduce the number of unexpected occurrences while the robot is working. The flow of people, vehicles, and items not involved in the robot's task is usually restricted.

traction friction between an object and the surface on which it moves, allowing the object to move without slipping.

unstructured environment in robotics, an area in which a robot operates that has not been specially designed for it. People, vehicles, and other things may pass through the area in which the robot works.

work envelope the area in which an industrial robot can reach and manipulate objects with its effector.

Index

A

actuators, 8, 17
aircraft: autopilot in, 34-35; navigating, 30-31; robotic, 20-25, 32. *See also* drones
astronauts, robotic, 17
Amazon (company), 13
Aquanaut (robot), 30-31
aquatic robots, 26-31
Atlas (robot), 18-19
automated guided vehicles (AGV's), 10-15
autonomous mobile robots (AMR's), 10, 13, 14
autonomous underwater vehicles (AUV's), 28-29
autonomous vehicles. *See* self- driving cars
autonomy, 19, 29; in self-driving cars, 36-41
autopilot, 34-35

B

Boston Dynamics (company), 16, 19

C

cars. *See* self-driving cars
cargo ships, 26-27

D

dark rides, 14-15
Defense Advanced Research Projects Agency (DARPA) Robotics Challenge, 18, 44-45
drones, 5, 31; autonomous, 20-21, 24-25; remote control, 22-23

E

Eagle Ray (AUV), 29
Ehang EH216-S (drone), 21
endless tracks, 8-9, 16

F

forklifts, automated, 11, 13

G

General Motors, 41
Great Barrier Reef, 28

H

humanoid robots, 18-19

I

industrial robots, 6

L

lasers, 12, 36-37
lidar, 13, 36-37

M

military vehicles, 45
mobile robots, 4-5; DARPA challenge for, 44-45; navigation by, 32-33

N

Nauticus Robotics (company), 31
navigation, 12-13, 32-33

O

omni wheels, 8-9

P

pallets, 10, 11, 22-23
Proteus (robot), 13

R

RangerBot (AUV), 28
RoboNation, 46-47

S

SeaPerch, 46-47
self-driving cars, 36-37; DARPA and, 44-45; degrees of autonomy in, 38-43; safety and benefits of, 42-43; sensors, 36-37
shipping, 26-27
simultaneous localization and mapping (SLAM), 32-33
SpotMini (robot), 16
structured environments, 6, 320

T

theme parks, 14-15
towing vehicles, or tuggers, 11

U

uncrewed aerial vehicles (UAV's). *See* drones
unstructured environments, 7

V

Valkyrie (robot), 17

W

walking robots, 16-19, 44
watercraft, robotic, 26-31
WaveGlider (robot), 28-29
wheels, 8-9, 16
work envelopes, 7

Y

Yara Birkeland (ship), 27

Z

Zipline (company), 5

[48]

www.ingramcontent.com/pod-product-compliance
Lightning Source LLC
Chambersburg PA
CBHW061254170426
43191CB00041B/2426